Bountiful Buffet

New and Collected Poems

Nathan Polsky

Volume 2

First Edition: December 2013
Printed in the United States of America
ISBN: 978-1-939237-18-7

Cover Art

"Sienna & Turquoise Color Blocks" by Debbie Dannheisser
Fine Art Gallery, www.DebbieDannheisser.com

To

Janet

Foreword

This year I'm committed to looking for joy in everything I see or do. It was easy to find joy in reading Nathan Polsky's poetry, the first volume, *Meaningful Sounds*, and the second volume, *Bountiful Buffet*.

As with all poetry, these poems will touch you in unique and individual ways, depending on how your life relates to the topics.

Part of the joy of reading *Bountiful Buffet* is the clear sense that Polsky, at age ninety, is brimming with joy and satisfaction as he reminisces and creates verse and rhyme on a variety (bountiful buffet?) of subjects – love, home, youth, old age, puppies, technology, children, and the fate of mankind.

Polsky's perspective gives rise to rich imagery – "Let's Reminisce" (As memories invade like album pages…visions yield to regrets and sighs...) And "One Person's Tale" (Please come to my party and say hello to old times…Let's gather for our last goodbye…Let's see the faces we looked at before…and talk about our past with a sigh.)

While there are glimpses into Polsky's personal life, most of the poems are thoughtful commentary on subjects everyone can relate to, and many are whimsical and add to the fun of reading the collection. "Gosh and Gee!" (We say 'Ta-Ta' when we leave a friend…and 'Ho-Hum' if we are bored…It's 'Ah-Ha' if we discover truth…and 'When!' when liquor's poured.)

Authentic and inspired, Polsky's poetry reminds me that when one calls upon their muse it can bring joy to self and others.

E. Marie Oberle, Ed.D., Author

Author's Note

Following the Volume I collection of poems, *Meaningful Sounds*, it is a pleasure to offer this Volume 2, *Bountiful Buffet*, hoping to share these additional thoughts and observations, in rhyme and other formats.

Whether serious or funny, this new collection will entertain, be thought-provoking and hopefully, insightful.

Life is filled with unlimited subjects, and, combined with our own personal experiences, can form a treasure-trove of output.

Some of today's poetry can be deeply metaphorical and conceptual, and, although beautifully written, can be hard to follow or digest.

I, therefore, choose to mostly rhyme and simplify for greater ease of the sharing experience.

Nathan Polsky

Contents

The Daily Walk

What a jolly sight when dog meets dog
and tails begin to wag,
and hello's said with shiny eyes
to see familiar tags.

They talk about the day's events,
the tidbits in their dish,
and this blessed opportunity
to greet as one would wish.

The gossip shared makes time go by
'til the leash begins to pull,
as owners part and start for home
all having had their full.

Tomorrow is another day
unless a saddening rain
cuts short the trip and social time
with wishes all in vain.

continued...

On longer walks when strange dogs meet
and routines don't apply,
there's sniffing and dog judgments made
before one senses "Hi!"

It's not as if all dogs are friends
the moment paths are crossed,
for we all know that we do the same:
it's peace or tempest-tossed!

It could be turf, it could be size,
it could be foul of mood,
if dogs could smile and say "hello!"
they wouldn't be so rude.

A Friendly Hint

Watching dogs who meet is fun,
to see their tails say "Hi!"
Their tails wave briskly like a fan,
we humans look and sigh.

Would it not be nice to see
a wagging human tail
when greeting friends to say "Hello!"
(how did nature fail?)

Our feelings would, of course, be seen
since strangers won't receive
this telling sign of greeting's warmth,
something they must achieve.

There are some bones at our spine's base,
a vestigial tail now lost,
which might have made our live less grim,
with hardly any cost.

It is a lot like shaking hands
or kissing on the cheek,
a Howdy-do!", so natural,
a wagging tail does speak.

Maze

Life is this amazing maze
into which we're pushed so soon:
In we go, the game begins.
It starts with mother's croon.

The faulty paths and those dead ends,
we're completely on our own,
relying on our guides and luck
while facing the unknown.

So much of life, we soon find out,
depends on guess and choice.
There's no way knowing what's ahead,
to cry or to rejoice.

We grow and play and go to school
(if we're the lucky ones).
The time will fly, our selves will form
alongside many suns.

Our early hints with home and gene
all share our history.
Our friends and foes, our health and falls,
add to the mystery.

Our major steps of job and mate
will help define our lot.
The good and bad will join our path,
The trick is to fear not.

So, given what we started with,
within our personal maze,
I wish all luck and best of all,
happy exciting days.

PASSERS-BY

I see you, yet I know you not,
your "you-ness" mystifies.
You fill my sight as you pass by
eclipsing "me's" and "my's."

It makes me wonder who you are
and what your purpose is,
your stride to where and what you'll do.
I give myself this quiz.

I try to guess your destined end
and why you hurry so.
Is there a chore or date to keep
with Joe or Jane or Moe?

Does hunger pull or time says rush
or bargains loom ahead?
Are you so late you cannot pause
and let yellow turn to red?

Whatever drives and sets your goal
you fill my city sight.
I am what you also see
when we both pause at the light.

Fortune Cookie Wisdom

Putting one's best foot forward is a rebuke to the other.
When in Rome, you worry about who's feeding the cat.
If you are on pins and needles, you probably
can't find a chair.
He who bites the bullet, will possibly break a tooth.
The phrase "You said a mouthful!" would make
a decent conversation difficult.

Swallowing your pride may be indicative of a
very hungry lion indeed!
The phrase "shoot the breeze" may be guaranteed
by the second amendment.
A wolf in sheep's clothing doesn't know where to shop.
A rose by any other name has thorns.
Nobody's prefect!

You can lead a horse to water, but can he swim?
A journey of a thousand miles calls for
comfortable walking shoes.
A seasoned veteran is worth his salt.
The best laid plans of mice and men
can be spoiled by a piece of cheese.
Sweeping things under the rug makes walking difficult!

He who fishes for compliments waits with baited breath.
As ye sew, so shall ye rip!
The first shall be last, if the last are armed.
He who sows wild oats
will have a memorable harvest, weather permitting

Pillow Talk Or From Bed To Verse

Now I lay me down to sleep...
(as I've heard it said)
brings peace to most, but not to me.
Instead I'm filled with dread.

This story's mine, I'll share it now,
you'll soon see why I sigh.
Your sleep is sound, you wake up new,
not me, I don't know why!

I've tried the counted sheep routine,
I've thought of happy days.
But the sound of ticks and tocks intrude
until the morning's rays.

I never sleep a wink at all.
I pray for shut-eye's peace.
I toss and wait for those 40 winks
and all those thoughts to cease.

I so desire sweet dream's allure
in the land of Nod's caress.
Instead, night's mare snorts loud and taunts
and makes the night a mess.

If bed bugs bite I'd surely know
(insomnia does that, you know.)
I listen nightly for the crack of dawn
or for the rooster's crow.

Others brag of their restful snoozes
and sleep 'til the call to wake.
But their rise and shine and up and at ′em
my own sad contrasts make.

To turn off the spigot of my active mind
what levers should I pull?
I dredge the past and friends 1ong gone,
My memory bank is full.

So, sleep-deprived I re-live what was
of battles won and lost
and review what's past and make new plans
and pay the sleepless cost.

On bed of bricks or feathered foam
the movie's scenes do flicker
with paths not taken, mistakes undone
(with the script I cannot dicker.)

The clock's hands make their hourly pass
while I toss and turn and hope
that what's past just goes and leaves me be
...or I'm at the end of my rope!

I yearn for peaceful slumber's bed
with breathing full and deep.
It's not the place for life's review
but only dreams to keep.

Departure

Of all the ills we're subject to
as lives advance with age,
there's few we fear with such remorse
as brain's loss of every page.

Our memory bank, our living's pasts
escape and disappear
into a void of nothingness:
it's a misery and worst fear!

When all is said and truth to tell,
our minds are who we are.
It's what we've done and know compressed
which makes our solo star.

Descending into this pit of hell,
where who we are is lost,
our precious self 's no longer there:
we're bankrupt by the cost.

It seems that Nature's claim on us
is being called as due.
We've lived our lives on borrowed time:
now make way for the new.

But when senses slowly slide away
and curtain's shade descends,
it breaks one's heart to watch and see
the loss of mate and friends.

Some lives of parents, siblings, too,
are emptied bit by bit,
like draining through a devilish sieve:
to witness this takes grit!

The body stays, but now who's there
but an empty remnant shell.
I hope such ills will never come:
but luck and time will tell.

Here And Now

We heat and cool when we desire,
a button and it's done.
We cook on stoves with knobs that turn,
our lives are easy fun.

We wash and dry with simple help
that plugs into the wall.
We dine from frozen packaged foods,
no pots to clean at all.

Our TV set is always there
to make us laugh or cry,
to entertain and tell us news
and tell us what to buy.

When nature calls and we respond,
no need for cold retreat.
Our comfort's need is dear and near,
our system can't be beat.

It's dark no more when in or out,
a switch can do the trick.
No torch or flame to light our way.
Now there's a trick that's slick!

No need for drums to send our voice
or courier's fastest horse,
our little phone, both cell and fixed,
can do without the Morse.

And when we want to go from here
to nearby shops or malls,
our autos, bus or trains will do.
Our lives just have no walls.

For further trips we fly like birds,
(will wonders never cease?)
inventive minds give ease and play,
(now why not invent peace?)

Such is our life and times today,
we take it all in stride,
and seldom think how far we've come
and should be filled with pride.

No king or lord of olden days
could boast as we can now.
They'd look at us and all we have
and enviously say "WOW!"

Lament

All through our lives they come and go,
the friends and pals and foe
to give the context to our years
and teach us what we know.

We see them all, the good and bad,
and selfish knaves at work
who take and take and me, me, me;
we stumble where they lurk.

They care alone for self and ease
no matter who they harm.
They come like scythes into the wheat
or get their fill through charm.

Like mines that burst along our path
if innocents wrongly walk,
the lack of warning signs abets
the feast of sharks that stalk.

With clever wit or words that soothe
somehow it seems to be
that all the best and joys of earth
are theirs for all to see.

They're there behind the shrub and tree
with documents and pen,
with smile and tie and shirttail tucked,
(will honor come - and when?).

The greed that eats away our trust
and makes unfairness plain,
tells much of real world's unkind face
and innocent victims' pain.

Glimpses

Some days are problem-racked and hard
and long for joyous comfort's hand
but elsewhere's needs demand it, too.

Misty dark shields moonlight's cry
for peace and kiss of kindness soft
and feathery stroke to ease the loss.

A burden's heft aloft some heads
makes life itself a cynic's proof
that asks again for Fate's reply.

A sorry tale indeed we note
when troubled souls abound about
with none to help or eyes that shut.

Is this the best that living's gift
can offer here on earthly ground
while passing time ignores and hides?

There's plenty here to go around
but systems' tilt avoids the choice
and take and thrive and live for few.

Some day ahead when ruination comes
and slates are clean and start anew
man's mind and need will love and share.

Ease and bliss await for most
as cherished ends and dreamer's sleep:
sweet tales to tell when once awake.

Twenty-Six

Imagine language's gift to us,
letters just twenty-six,
for all we read and hold to heart
comes from this simple mix.

Our books and what we write and speak
owe all to twenty-six.
Our native tongues and deepest minds
need no more fancy tricks.

From early on to yesterday,
these letters were combined,
in countless ways by sage and wit
to create our common mind.

These twenty-six combined at will,
each letter used as brick,
helped build our cultural edifice
and made our progress tick.

So homage pay for all we know,
to letters sparse and few,
assembled well to guide our world
and enlighten me and you.

Let's mix and match these twenty-six
our deepest thoughts to tell,
and add our own to what is there
our ignorance to quell.

Low Point

There are some times when luck is bad
and plans go up in smoke.
There's nothing we can say or do
but laugh at fortune's joke.

It's what it is, you softly say,
and wipe away the tear
as disappointment clouds the eyes
and so you say "Oh, dear."

You look forlorn and feel the hurt,
your self-esteem is low.
Que sera, sera, you shrug and say
and just go with the flow.

So it goes, you meekly think,
I just give up for now.
What's the use, I've tried my best,
my fate just won't allow.

And that's the way it is for now,
the way the cookies crumble.
So be it, and that's life, you say,
go figure, you just mumble.

Life is just what it is, you say,
a fine how-do-you-do!
What will be, will be, God only knows
(but I've had my winnings, too.)

Well, what are you gonna do, my friends,
when luck just knocks you down.
Your timing's late, the hands don't turn,
breathe deep and just don't drown.

There must be reason for such blows.
(I hear others say the same.)
If it's rolling dice and numbered wheel,
I'll play another game.

I mustn't give up, but try again
and wipe my knees and eyes.
Tomorrow's sun will shine, I hope.
The past has made me wise!

Second Chance

The marvel of our age, it seems,
the wondrous gift of all,
is when we have a broken part
we visit a medical mall.

If your heart fails, you need not fret,
with luck a new one's there.
If kidneys balk or livers sass
we know to go for care.

Replacing teeth is not a chore,
our smile is there to see.
A new hip waits to ease your walk
to buy your Tetley tea.

When hairlines merge with nape of neck
and mirrors smirk and taunt,
our skillful art and salesmanship
enables you to flaunt.

No need to worry if knees go bad,
another just waits for you.
The miraculous skills of bright MDs
can fix that problem, too.

When breathing with our lungs is hard,
they've found a way to cure:
Replace the blasted haggard ones
and you'll be fine, for sure!

Ligaments, joints and muscles, too,
our mechanics can repair.
And if your mind and brain go soft
replace it, if you dare!

They can lift a face and remove the crease
and give a tummy tuck;
a bit of liposuction, too,
if one just has the buck!

Our hearing aids will also help
when nature's work is weak.
Our eyeglass lens will improve our sight,
and help to regain our peak!

Now if only we can push time back
to where we smugly were,
and start anew with glint in eye
and escape our old age slur!

For Sale

Everything's for sale, it seems,
we've pushed the limit far.
There is no end to what is sold,
our age has raised the bar!

Whatever named, to use or own,
describes our salesmen's pitch.
But it's strange to see a novel trend,
what can be bought when rich!

A little cash, a big bequest
will buy you what was free.
Your name can shine in letters bold
for all the world to see.

Above the arch and rooftop's height
your name will impress our eyes,
to tell us all what money's for,
and that's the ultimate prize.

In times gone by, a famous man
had earned the honor rare,
with talent, rank or impressive deed
or gifts bestowed with flair.

But if now you pay and promise more,
you have the naming right,
your name remembered for all time
by day and every night.

So, school or hall or field or road,
or stadium, park or lab,
their name is there for all to see
if they pick up the tab.

As cities starve for funds to thrive
an opportunity awaits,
to change the map's familiar names
to those of nouveau greats.

Escape

A sponge that's square with eyes and mouth,
a mouse that's fun to hear,
an elephant's flight, a talking cow,
they're all our peers, though queer.

They joke and dance and sing for us
and do become our friends.
They also teach the younger ones
that learning never ends.

They amuse, amaze and evade what's real
through fantasy's open door.
They make us laugh or bring a smile.
Our children beg for more.

But that's not enough, by far, you see.
Just look who's protecting us:
those capes or masked and muscle-bound
bring peace without a fuss.

They fly at will (how is it done?)
they jump up to the moon.
They bring to justice all that's bad.
They help us none too soon.

The villains, crooks and evil ones
should know their fates are sealed.
With fighting, climbing men and gals
our wounds will all be healed.

We've become a cartoon society,
our children, and us, as well.
It's pure escape from real world things.
I'm for it. Can't you tell?

A Happy Solution

There once was a rabbit (some children say wabbit)
who lived all alone near a tree.
But he had a bad habit, this live-alone rabbit,
that bothered others, not me.

He sang in the morning when the sun first appeared.
He sang after lunch, as well.
He sang after dinner and before going to bed,
and also to the stars, truth to tell.

His voice was not bad for a little white bunny:
but he didn't know when to stop.
A song or two would have been nice to hear,
but his songs kept up with his hop.

His neighbors complained and tried to be nice,
for, after all, a song was no crime.
They said he should learn to lower his voice:
or try writing poems that would rhyme.

He wanted to please, but he just found it hard.
He tried singing softly and low.
He sang in the spring when buds would appear
until acorns would drop and winds blow.

This couldn't go on; it was disturbing the peace,
until someone had an idea that was great.
Why not have everybody join in the singing?
The neighbors could hardly wait!

They asked the old owl to help form the group,
and asked the rabbit to lead.
The "Neighborhood Singers" became known far and wide!
What a solution to a neighborhood's need!

One Person's Tale

As memories invade like album pages,
visions yield to regrets and sighs
for long-gone youth and silent rages,
abounding melancholic cries.

The soulful search, those tears of dreams,
facing mysteries and mist;
and worlds so vaporous, it seems,
preventing my brow be kissed.

I cried my tears, forlorn and sad,
(I never spoke of this in shame)
except that once with sorrow clad
a stranger sought to explain the game.

"To find your place in the scheme of things,
to fit into the waiting s1ot,
takes strength and growth of sturdy wings!"
She gently said "I kid you not!"

Albeit slow, the years passed by,
my silent self accepted most,
yet standing by, still asking "why?"
and living a stranger's void as host.

A comfort zone was yet to come
as shed coats made way for 1ife;
what seemed so real, impressing some,
still masked the loner's strife.

How many snows and suns have passed,
war and jobs have come and left
(my wife and girls helped time go fast)
we coped with burdens' heft.

The advancing clock marks journey's end,
we watch as memories fade,
I finally see myself as friend:
with life and soul my peace is made.

Sweet Treat

Oh, the soothing taste of a chocolate bar,
candy or chocolate cake;
that brown, delicious, yummy treat.
When deprived, I start to shake.

There are so few things that please me more,
and gives me so much pleasure.
It sits upon my tongue when eaten,
and becomes a melting treasure.

So, others may have their spice or tart,
which puzzles me a lot,
but who's to say what pleases some:
of my chocolate, deprive me not!

The Useful Drawer

Can you imagine how we ever got by
without the useful drawer:
this sliding, pulling, simple space
in which to hide, collect or store!

Taken for granted without a thought,
wherever we work or live,
drawers keep everything out of sight,
until it's asked to give.

They're big or small and all around,
beneath a counter, desk or table.
We get to know where all things are,
even without a label.

I not only speak of kitchen things,
or clothing, towels and such,
but also what we might call junk
and don't appreciate much.

Drawers do help to separate
things we save or need,
which are part of life's necessities
and seem to accumulate and breed.

It might be called a doo-dad place,
but such drawers do make a home,
for one never knows what's needed when,
so, let's honor them with this poem.

I Hope It's Not Catching!

My nose is stuffed, my eyeballs hurt,
my pittering heart won't patter.
My ears can't catch the low-pitched voice
My wife asks, "What's the matter?"

My bones, they creak, my toes are cold,
I feel my temperature rise.
My tongue is white, my cough gets worse,
my ankles grow in size.

My aching back prevents my sleep
(a tooth joins in the fun!)
My skin is many shades of red,
I feel my life is done!

My tingling toes play drumming tunes,
my stomach makes such sounds.
A headache comes to pay respects
and join the baying hounds.

I'm short of breath, I can't walk far,
my feet just feel like Jell-O.
I've got to rest and catch my breath,
arthritis says "Hello!"

My watery eyes and leaking nose
suggest I'm going to die,
but then I hear a voice within:
"We are experiencing technical difficulties. Please stand by!"

Hello And Good-Bye

It's odd that friends and newly met
all ask about my health.
They seem to care, if words mean much
(but not about my wealth.)

Their greeting always is the same,
they ask me, "How are you?"
Sometimes the newer ones I meet
will say, "How do you do?"

When leaving them and going home
some will say, "Take care!"
as if a creature on the street
would take me to its lair.

Some may say, "You're looking well!"
Some others wouldn't dare
to tell the truth if I look sick
(honesty is so rare!).

Some friends instead of "How are you?"
will shorten it to "Hi!".
When leaving, some are merchant types
who always say "Buy! - Buy!"

I often do the same, you know:
it's part of our social gene.
We greet and leave in patterned ways,
but it's really what we mean.

Have a nice day!

Small World

I remember kids' tin cans and strings,
how clever we were then!
The telephone was a nerdy tool,
with luck, each block had ten!

It seemed so strange to hear a voice
(and someone heard me, too!)
How could a sound so fill a wire,
I really had no clue.

Our world would change as time went by
and daring brains and skill
would make us faint with joy and pride,
for progress is not still!

But as the world became so small
with talk and song and print
that come from tiny magic things,
what's next…I want a hint!

Every day brings new surprise,
we cannot wait to see
what brings us close and stays in touch,
for tomorrow's a mystery.

I've never seen such need to talk
and death to silent peace;
for when we leave the house at morn
our friendships cannot cease.

Some day we'll no longer need this tool
or gadgets unborn still.
We'll find a way to think and call!
How far this is from quill!

Nostalgic Noodles

The old Chinese waiter came with the place.
We had gone there for years and years
and have enjoyed this ethnic island
of the obligatory wanton soup,
lobster Cantonese, dessert of ice cream
over pineapple chunks
and, of course, the almond cookie
with hot tea.

This enticing stomach-soothing treat,
in memory, is not complete without
that shuffling, elderly server
with pad, pencil and arm-draped
white linen napkin.

His order-taking was without emotion,
his eyes downcast and his mind elsewhere,
as this routine was repeated, undoubtedly,
hundreds of times a month.
He was a silent, distant figure,
somehow related to the hanging red lanterns
and good luck Chinese calligraphy
posters and banners, providing
the requisite touches of a foreign adventure.

Of course, he has long been gone.
But it is sweet reminiscing on this oh, so young,
nostalgic memory when such visual sights and flavors
entered our younger pores.

No Choice

I love to see the kids at play,
their squeals of merriment,
cutting through the dull of day,
remembering joy that went.

They run and shout as puppies do,
God bless their excess zeal.
I watch and wish I joined them, too,
for that to me is real.

I long to run and shout aloud:
but the clock and joints say nay.
I cannot join the scootered crowd,
today's not yesterday.

If not my search for daily bread,
if not my making's cage,
I, too, would run but my body said:
it's past your time and age.

My own remembered youth and joy
could match and join this bunch;
I, too, once had my wheels and toy
but now I just eat lunch.

I cannot now just race and throw,
life's grip will not permit.
I cannot lean against the flow:
I watch, and here just sit.

Guiding Lights

While driving down a street last week
I had to stop at lights:
those hanging colored orbs that stare
and function days and nights.

They tell you when to stop and go
and when to slow your speed.
Their function's clear for safety's sake
...signals we're glad to heed.

But then the thought occurred to me,
that our lives need such a guide
to help define the roads we take
for a smoother, stress-free ride.

Consider if these colored lights,
those three that ease our way,
were also there in our life's mode
to help us day to day.

The red, of course, would tell us stop
and not to take a chance.
The green would say it's fine to go,
our project to enhance.

The yellow warns to slow and think
and cautiously proceed,
and weigh the chances and the odds
and not succumb to greed.

So, to stop and go or do not rush,
is advice we really need,
the "yes" and "no" and "maybe" guides
to help us with our deed .

A great idea, if I must say,
behind which I will stand.
Timid or daring or thoughtless acts,
such lights would guide our hand!

Layman's Debt

I feel we're getting ever close
to the mysteries we face,
those corners dark and unexplored
that victimize our race.

I try so hard to understand
what science tries to do
to help us live a better life,
just how, I have no clue

The words they use to share their work
are much too deep for me.
It's foreign talk among themselves:
a lock without a key.

I feel left out as you will, too:
just try to get the gist!
It's not that we are dumb or daft,
just lost in haze and mist.

So here's the test to check your wit:
see whether you can pass,
and if you do much better than I,
don't give me any sass!

The minimal reaction optimization
hyper-condensation,
idiopathic pulmonary fibrosis,
lymphocyte activation.

Signaling molecules sequestration,
precursor exocytosis,
cytoplasmic proteins,
unheralded mitosis.

No effect on mitotic progression
or cellular viability,
negative activation entropy
and high processivity.

With phosphorylitic onelcoartivator
and binary omissions shown,
when studying disease parthogenesis
or the anaphase spindle alone.

So with non-specific amplification
and primer degradation,
the reaction-diffusion properties
have multiple application.

continued…

The tyrosine autosphorylation
with the transcription factor
significantly increased by stimulation
is the important actor.

The jet of relativistic particles
and polarized gamma-ray photons,
emission synchrotron radiation,
displaying the positive protons.

I'll just assume the future's sure,
the brains among us thrive.
The work goes on in quiet quest
...let's give them all high five!

So, wondrous science does impress,
with language hard to scan
We may not share vocabulary,
but I am its greatest fan!

Family Way

Not long ago I read somewhere
of robots being built,
that'll sweep a room or take out trash:
all creatures without guilt.

These plastic things will mix a drink
or sing a lusty tune
or even cook an evening meal
(I really want one soon!).

No need to shave or buy it shoes,
it only asks to serve.
It stays or goes just as we wish
(I think I'll call mine "Merv").

No need to walk it like a pet
or feed it doggie chow.
I'll teach it tricks and play some games.
I wish I had one now.

With computer discs and metal parts,
wires, lights and sound,
someday we'll all have one of these
and think it's heaven-found.

But if it stops with battery dead
and doesn't do as bid,
we'll just play God and plug it in,
my wife's and my new kid!

Attachment

The button, laces, hook and eye,
the knot and zipper, too,
were marvels of ingenious use
with special jobs to do.

A sash or string or clip or clasp,
these all we use and know,
snap and bow, a bead or loop:
these make for status quo.

We've seen such things at work, of course,
they make for living's ease.
We do not give a second thought
when used in heat or freeze.

But I do reserve my hearty cheer
when fastening that to this:
it's nature's burr, that nuisance plant,
giving us a Velcro® kiss!

Loving Travelers

I am me, and you are you,
sometimes we are as one.
I itch, you scratch, your thirst is mine.
We always share the fun.

I know the way your mind is set,
you know my hunger's time.
I know your projects' aim and hopes,
you read and like my rhyme.

We tread the path and roam the roads,
we share what comes our way.
The years have sewn our skins as one
as sun and moon make day.

Our gift to life, if I may say,
our daughters represent.
We've added and enriched the world
and lent meaning as was meant.

The breath comes slow and pain's not far,
what was we cannot do.
We walk with what is left of stride
and long for what was new.

I know the parade has got to stop,
our day of marching ends.
I'll miss your pure and gentle heart.
Alone, we'll still be friends.

Voyage

From start to end our life unfolds
from baby to old age.
We grow and play and find our way
within this mortal cave.

We learn about the world around
which looks askance at you
and learn to love and trust or run
or stay and stir the brew.

Our mirror tells us how we age
as years fly by and taunts,
at failures and right paths forsook
(the memory surely haunts!).

We do our bit within our reach
as best we can contrive.
We work, we wed, we parent well,
ambition makes us strive.

With luck and chance to guide our way
around the cracks and ruts,
we trip and fall and rise again,
despite the bruise and cuts.

So living's trials and varied jobs
combine with joy and pain,
and friends that come and go away:
such is our loss and gain.

Our bottom line is where we are,
just gazing at our gray.
The creaks and stiffening joints announce:
December is not May!

Our being's wheels are slowing down,
I sense the station's near.
All told, we tried and loved and now
there's nothing more to fear.

Nature's Helpers

We've come a long way, it is said,
when life was short and hard;
but now we have amazing tools,
our cherished youth to guard.

Let's think about our body's care,
the time we fuss and preen,
to repair and soften aging's flight
and keep our beings clean.

Our mirrors speak with guile-less truth,
our nose betrays us, too.
We no longer roam in furry pelts:
we know now what to do.

We shower, rinse and wash away,
and gargle, brush and comb.
We tweeze and shave and trim our hair
before we leave our home.

We tint and dye and lubricate,
we spray and pluck and squeeze;
We wax and powder, pick and rub
and our perfume joins breeze.

We color lips and color hair;
we smear and sometimes polish.
We deodorize, massage and paint;
all calendars to abolish.

The daily rites of daily care
demand so much of time.
I could not resist to remind us all,
and summarize with rhyme.

Deceiving Silence

Our living space is not empty and silent:
but a boiling soup of voices, words and pictures,
and waves of energy enveloping us,
requiring only the appropriate receiver
to fully complete access to mission and purpose.

The future's arrival will overwhelm and control:
with nature and man at coming mercies.

Machines and devices prevailing today
are infants overshadowed by tomorrow.

Unfair

The game is over when the winners' bounty
collects all cards and marbles
and offers most others
dregs and dross....and only enticing hope.

The Source

What insights into society's ills
are found if one knows where to look.
We yearn for enlightenment on matters so grave,
and discovered a philosopher's book.

It's readily available at a nominal cost
with pictures and. many a deep thought.
It circulates widely and encourages talk
and contains information long sought.

The authors know much and solemnly write;
their readers devour their advice.
They share secrets and knowledge and news of the day,
and all for an affordable price.

I'll review some of the items I've recently read
which helped define meaning of life.
I now am aware of the world that exists:
I never knew of such insights and strife.

I learned of the parties and gossip and scandals,
the real scoop of who's in who's bed,
the break-ups, adultery, starlets and studs,
The wandering eye and well fed.

Divorces and sex and jealousies rampant,
lesbian, gay interludes;
kiss and tell stories and the lowdown on cheats,
call girls, strippers and nudes.

Five sure-fire ways to improve your IQ,
and slimming from a twelve to a six;
improving your love life with diet and make-up,
eight self-gratification new tricks.

How to get rid of wrinkles and flab;
controlling your destiny, too.
Nine ways to appeal to the opposite sex.
Read it and you'll know what to do.

You say you're not interested and don't believe a word,
like the secret of flattening your belly;
but the newsstands and counters scream loudly for your eyes,
like how to avoid buttocks like jelly.

So, craving advice and wisdom and joy,
this might be the source that you seek,
to learn from the masters who want only to help:
I recommend it with my tongue in my cheek.

Gosh And Gee!

We speak a language that's short and sweet,
that helps express our thought:
we use it all so naturally,
as if we're all self-taught.

It's what we say in daily life,
these colorful words and sound,
appropriate for it's moment's use,
and there's more yet to be found.

We say "TA-TA!" when we leave a friend,
and "HO-HUM", if we are bored.
It's "AH-HAH!" if we discover truth,
and "WHEN!" when liquor's poured.

"M-M-M-M…" is our pensive pause,
"BOO-HOO!" when crying and sad.
We say "PEE-YOO!" at odors ripe;
"DAMN!" if we're really mad.

"DUH!" makes fun at dumb remarks;
"BAH!" is a dismissive sound.
"WHACK-O!" is used for a crazy man,
"HOT DOG!" when money's found.

"OH, NO!" is said when something's wrong;
"HEY!" will get attention.
"OH, PULEEZE!" if we don't think it's funny,
"YUCK!" at things not to mention.

There's "SH-H-H!" if trying to hold down noise;
when feeling crummy, it's "BLAH".
You say "OH, YEAH?" if challenging one,
and a cheer is called a "RAH!"

"GR-R-R" is when you're really angry;
"TEE-HEE" is a subdued titter.
"HUSHHHH" is used to pacify a baby;
"EEK!" when seeing a small critter!

When stopping a horse, one just says "WHOA!";
and "OOPS!" if a glass should drop;
"TRA-LA-LA" when skipping through the grass,
"CRIPES!" if your play's a flop.

We say "HOORAY!" when our team wins;
"OH-OH!" when danger's near.
Men go "GA-GA" over a pretty girl,
and say "AH-H-H-H" with a hot day's beer.

Puzzled or confused, one might say "HUH?"
and a gift might make you say "WOW!".
"TOODLE-OO!" is said when it's time to go;
a right to the "KISSER" is "POW!".

"TOOTSIE" is a term of childish affection;
"TACKY" describes bad taste.
"MUSH!" is yelled at a dog-sled team.
A "BOO-BOO" results from haste!

continued…

"DRAT!" is said when patience gives out;
"UNCLE!" when losing a fray.
"OH, SHOOT!" is better than some other words,
"SHOO!" will chase chickens away.

We say "A-A-AH" for the doctor, "OUCH!" when it hurts;
"WHEW!" when the job's finally done.
We say "YUMMY!" when taste buds are especially pleased,
and say "YIPES!" at a lousy pun.

That "SO AND SO" is a disapproved person,
and "PHOOEY!" says it all!
"WHOOP-DE-DOO!" is easy come and go,
"WHOOP-EE!" if we have a ball!

When it's inconsequential, most might say "PIFFLE!";
"PISH-POSH!" dismisses as minor.
"POOF!" when anything is suddenly gone!
"CHEEZY" means cheap and not finer!

"PEEK-A-BOO!" is playing a game of hiding,
"TUT-TUT" will minimize;
"YOU-HOO!" is when we call from afar,
and "GEE WHISKERS!" we do like French fries!

When things go well, it's "OKEE-DOKEE";
when exasperated, we say "GAD-ZOOKS!"
It's "SCRAM!" when getting rid of pests,
and "JEEZ!" when we dislike our looks!

"BOO!" is when you suddenly frighten,
a "WHAMMY" gives someone bad luck.
We say "CHOP-CHOP!" when desiring speed,
"OH-OH!" when you are stuck!

It's "HUNKY-DORY" when things go your way,
and there are sunsets that call for an "OO-O-O-O!".
"OH, BROTHER!" speaks of your dismay or surprise,
and when sneezing, one says "AH-CHOO!"

A "LU-LU" could be a major mistake,
and it's "WHOOPS!" for a social blunder.
It's "YUCKY!" if the cheese is green,
and it's "HM-M-M-M" whenever you wonder.

We say "BR-R-R-R" when it's really cold,
"GODDAM!" if it gets too hot!
What you don't believe is a lot of "HOO-EY";
we say "KOOTCHY-KOO!" when befriending a tot!

"OH?" is a questioning, quizzical sound,
"YAK, YAK" is talking too much.
"LA-DEE-DAH!" is easy come, easy go,
and saying "GROOVY!" is such a nice touch!

So, that's my selection of expressions we use:
those bits of our lingual stew.
They ease our talk and express with "OOMPH!",
"BY GOLLY!" and what else is new?

Boxed Memory

What a joy it was
to open a new box of crayons,
and breathe in
the smell of the wax sticks!

And be thrilled
at the assortment of colors:
virginal and waiting!

It's a very special moment of memory,
for anyone in later years.

Positives And Negatives

What wonders yet await us
as nimble, focusing minds
follow the spurs of invention
and intuition.

What clever and dizzying prizes
await to bring ease and wellness,
convenience and comfort to all.

But the same ingenuity and fertility
will also direct themselves
to projects of domination, control,
destruction and death.

Technology and brains
serve two masters.

Short Story

Our very early years of life
are filled with learning's stares
at Mommy's face, at hanging toys
at plush and funny bears.

The warmth and cuddly arms are there
to lift and play with song,
the feeding times and carriage rides
just shout that "you belong!"

Then comes the day when crawling ends
and walking takes the stage.
Such fun to go from here to there
and time to turn the page.

So many things to see and do,
the days are short but sweet
discovering every blade of grass
and the thrill of walking feet.

As puppies romp and love to play,
so, too, the playtimes come.
The days are spent on rest and fun
(too soon to think of Prom!).

The schooling starts and birthdays pass,
the numbered candles grow,
as time takes flight with planet's spin
through suns and falling snow.

The years fly by and schooling ends
and adventures come and go,
with jobs to do to make a life:
a person's got to grow.

Then marriage looms and there's the joy,
Life's circle comes around.
The baby's trip from then to now
is Life's tape just re-wound.

These varied tales of Life's parade
is hard to briefly say.
Each baby's fate will just unfold
in every baby's way.

It's Quite Simple

Our brains and living systems
are but factories
to foster species' survival,

absorbing sustenance and energy
to sustain this priority

until inadequate age intrudes
and offers no secondary natural purpose.

Food For Thought

We're what we eat, we're always told,
so wouldn't it be fun
to see ourselves as fish or fowl
or meat that is well done.

A veggie dish would make us green,
a leg of lamb as brown.
This game is so amusing now,
I think I am a clown.

The plum and orange, grape and pear
lend color to my face,
and carrot, pea and celery stalk
would add an air of grace.

A liver chopped, a shrimp that's cooked,
a chicken's leg or breast
will help us make us what we are
and show us at our best.

I'll also eat the juicy foods
with a smoother surface flesh,
and hope my looks have real appeal:
always ripe and fresh!

Depression

My wife suggests my poems depress
and lack a happy tone.
I do agree, I'll tell you why.
I'm sure I'm not alone.

My pen could just plant flowery words
and overlook the bad,
but life is not just fragrant scents,
and misery makes me sad.

So many souls do try their best.
as I watch and read and see.
Is it Fate or Man that makes our mess?
I wish we found the key.

Throughout the ages (and now our own)
Too many starve and toil
to ease and please the strong and few:
does that make your blood boil?

We've got to see beyond ourselves,
and try to do what's right.
We're not alone through journey's ride
and accept another's plight.

So, yes, my wife is right to wish
that happy smiles caress
and all is sugary candy bars
(Me, too, I will confess!).

But let's be frank and see the truth:
that human hurt exists,
and no amount of "love" and "dove"
can provide evasive mists.

To many now, so safe and fed,
such thoughts disturb and gall.
Our sporty games and partied times
will not delay our fall.

So, "moon" and "June" and lollipops
are fine and give most fun.
My wife is right, I do depress
'til outer peace is won.

Questions

This pound or two of entwining mass
within our cranial bone
has developed to where we are right now
as Nature's might has shown.

Another million years or so,
what will a human be,
and how changed from what we are today?
I'd love to wait and see.

Evolution's march led to today:
we changed from cell to now,
from swimming things to lawyer kinds,
from low to higher brow.

Will man be taller than we are,
or still have hands and feet?
Will horns and claws predominate?
Will other forms compete?

His brain, I'm sure, will grow and thrive
to compute and Google well.
He'll think and it will all be done.
How, I cannot tell.

Flying wings may yet appear,
or eyes that see through steel,
or water-dwelling breathing tubes
when changed to live like seal.

Will men give birth and women rule
because they're large and strong?
And will the roach and ant prevail?
I hope I'm proven wrong!

Oh, to see so far ahead,
we know that change will be:
if earth still turns and sun still shines,
will there be a "we"?

Taking One's Chances

A baby's staring eyes
surveys you carefully,
until it is satisfied
that you would do it no harm.

Yours is a new image
to enter its world
and must be cautiously
checked out!

With such assurances, the ice is broken,
and a relationship
might be born.

Some don't wish to be disturbed
in their private world
and won't tolerate intrusions,
causing an immediate
verbal expression
of that view.

Peace On Earth

With absolute certainty, presumption and conceit
some people know God's truths, intent,
appearance, image…even location…
and that they alone possess the magic key,
path and password.to heavenly bliss
and eternal life.

They feel the urgent mission to share
their belief with all…with reason or blood.
Their path is the true and only one,
dictating behavior, dress, diet,
head's hair growth and cover, ritual,
sexual domination and very specific time
and methods for pleading and worship,
for they are specially chosen gate-keepers,
appropriately dressed, to prevent direct contact
with the divine and creator, except through them,
their prophets, saints, messengers and their books
of dogma and tales.

What mayhem, torture, destruction, corpses, cruelty
and domination this world has endured
in enforcing obedience to the dictates
of self-appointed hierarchies, or self-anointed.
The competition for saving "souls" will yet destroy us.

My Darling Janet

I count my lucky days and stars,
as the saying goes,
when first I saw and met this girl
(who knew I would propose?)

Her beauty shone and struck my heart
(I was so timid then.)
I never thought she'd later yield
and select me among men.

Our life as team can fill a book
through all the ups and downs.
We've followed jobs around a lot
to cities and to towns.

She stayed and showed her loyal love
through failure and success,
without complaint or bitterness,
ignoring pain's duress...

Others might have left for good,
my Janet stood her ground.
My partner and support through all
'til slowly peace was found.

My love for her compounds with time,
appreciation abounds:
She is my best friend and my home,
as simple as that sounds.

She's clever, cute, perceptive, wise
and my lovely children's mother:
creative, smart and sensitive
and generous as no other.

Her council wise, her insights deep,
we've pulled as team together.
I love her more as aging creeps,
no ifs or buts or whether!

So here I sit and put to words
my affection and my joy
at joining Janet from my youth:
I'm such a lucky boy!

A Message From Your Friendly Banker

If you read and understand the small type print
on the back of any form sent to you recently,
our relationship is null and void.

We reserve the right for whatever reason
to restate the interest rate on your account.
We also reserve the right to accept your money,
for which little or no interest will be paid,
with the understanding that we will buy, sell, invest, trade,
etc., and so forth, in any way or manner we wish, and retain
whatever gain is realized.
Any loss experienced by us in connection with
such unencumbered use of your funds,
will be reimbursed to us by bailout or surcharges.

Also, you are reminded of the increased fees
for any of the forty reasons which were recently sent to you,
which includes late payment fees, overdraft fees,
inactivity fee, check writing, check cashing,
office remodeling, cost of living adjustment, staff bonuses,
office expenses, (i.e. telephone, paper, coffee),
expenditures for contributions to political bundlers,
and any legal expenses incurred in connection
with safeguarding our interest, whatever they are.

Also, if you choose to pay the minimum
as shown on your bill,
you are a stupid person.

As a further condition for accepting our terms,
you must include us in your daily prayers.
We are here to serve. God bless America!

Good Old Days

Those good old days when time was young,
and often wrapped in fun,
are remembered now with perfect thought,
and the bad we forget or shun.

We think of chirping birds and sun,
vacations, friends and games;
the jokesters and the characters
(we're good at forgetting names).

Sometimes it's rare that good old days
were without a hurt or scars.
Our minds adjust and wrap from view
things that perfection mars.

It's a mind-set game that does no harm:
our fiction grows with age.
There's solace in those carefree years,
for it brightens our present cage.

Moving Image

The god-light from behind
passes through our imaged plastic film
projecting for all to see
who we are:

Our weakness, frailty, strengths,
growing, dying
and all in-between
with occasional joy accompanying
pain, sorrow, departures,
juiced with hopes, ambitions, dreams
begging for Mentor and Muse
to guide and empower,
scything away the weedy, pestilent ivy,
scabrous underbrush, seeking
to entangle stumbling feet.

The screen, our viewed persona,
is the reality for judgment,
ripe for plaudits,
Parental Guidance only,
rave or rout.

Good Taste

Condiments help our food taste good:
they add that zing or tang.
Tastes vary so among us all,
mild, to spicy bang!

The ketchup's there and also salt,
alongside the pepper shaker;
there's mustard and horseradish, too,
and sugar for the tea taker.

Every culture seasons food:
juices, leaves or powder,
garlic, cloves, tabasco, chile,
curry for the chowder.

Nutmeg, saffron, ginger, spice,
cinnamon, paprika embellish:
all of these enhancing flavors
lend meaning to "eat with relish"!

Extend this thought to life, itself,
seasoned with love or play:
enriching days with peace and friends,
keeping the dark at bay!

The Humble Egg

A chicken's eggs are welcomed food,
our mornings have a choice:
and for omelette lovers everywhere
I'm among those who rejoice!

There's choice of hard or soft-boiled eggs,
fully fried or over easy;
perhaps with sausage or bacon strips,
plain or maybe cheesy.

Chopped onion cooked with scrambled eggs
add flavor to gild the lily.
There's Western and Spanish styles, as well,
with ketchup or some chili.

Let's not forget egg salads, too.
There are so many variations:
combined with veggies on rye or toast,
I applaud the chef's creations.

Eggs Benedict's a favorite of mine,
on an English muffin bed,
eaten with hash browns and some juice,
it fortifies the week ahead!

So, thank you, hens, for all your gifts
to help supplement cereals and flakes.
Your talents are very impressive to us:
you've certainly got what it takes!

Unfinished

There's so much more I'd like to do,
before the whistle blows:
projects lined awaiting time;
my impatience only grows.

My mind is filled with great ideas,
for rhymes or art and thought;
I won't waste precious time to brood
about past battles fought.

I am here now as ripened fruit,
subject to nature's whim:
before, with silent snap or moan,
my eyes and self grow dim.

But, while senses still exist and rule,
insights are there to share;
and nimble fingers have not yet forgotten
to creatively express and care.

Comparative

Do you want to know what trouble is?
Oh, boy! You shouldn't ask!
I hope bad luck wouldn't recognize me
if I were to wear a mask!

My bunions hurt, my ankles swelled,
I'm putting on so much weight.
My hair is thinning, and turning gray,
and my daughter's period is late!

The loan I wanted was just turned down,
my credit card was refused;
I broke a tooth at lunch today:
believe me, I'm not amused!

My Venetian blind broke when I pulled:
I hate that blasted thing!
My refrigerator leaks like hell;
my door bell doesn't ring!

I sprained my back when lifting books.
My boss said he might close.
My son says he'll run away:
it could be worse, I suppose!

My toilet bowl just overflowed,
my wife wants a divorce.
My broker says I lost a lot,
but he says he has remorse!

My car needs tires and transmission, too;
I had to have it towed.
With arthritis in my joints, you see,
I'm bearing quite a load!

I think of running away somewhere
to some island where it's warm;
but with my luck, I fear I'll be eaten
by a ravenous mosquito swarm!

What's that, you say? You can match me in spades?
Your tumor has just returned?
Your leg had to be cut off, you've lost sight in one eye?
No, I didn't know your home was burned!

You need a liver transplant now?
Your insurance won't cover the cost!
Your ear drum burst just last week?
And the sight in your left eye was lost?

You're going to jail for insider trading?
You're being sued for every cent you've got?
Gee, I really should keep my big mouth shut.
I think I'll accept my own lot!

Fortune's Whim

As our life's aging stream
endlessly flows forward,
we remember delicious tastes, mother's food,
games played, sounds, scenes, streets,
friends, school, jobs, family, homes:
whatever was present in our younger days.

As we age, we think of these earlier times:
it's disappointments, surprises,
characters entering and leaving our lives,
our first this, our first that, our failures,
our successes, fears,
pivotal turning points and decisions,
memories sweet (or not!),
loss and events better forgotten.

The flickering film unwinds,
and is always available for re-showing, at will,
until the descending shade, at fortune's whim,
dims the light and we blankly stare
at the strangers at our side.

Slowly, soundlessly, inexorably,
knowing becomes unknowing.
There is no past, just a puzzling present.
Our container of essence, identity and memory
is empty.

White-Out

Perfection is elusive,
dogging our days and attacking without pity
our self-esteem and error-prone pride.

But man's clever, ingenious
and inventive wit has timely salvaged
our self-inflicted wounds
...with correction fluid!

It's great for our typing;
but, wouldn't it be marvelous
if we possessed a human equivalent:
a correction fluid,
that would erase our life's mistakes,
providing us with a second chance?

Don't Hang Up!

For so many commercial and personal reasons,
the telephone is a useful tool:
it gives convenience to our lives.
We've always thought it cool.

But like some friends, it has its faults,
this system of communication:
annoying habits, delays and such,
which causes irritation.

But, indeed, since it's added much,
We tolerate and endure.
The list below is the price we pay:
And I hope there is some cure!

Please hold for the next available representative.
Your call is very important to us. Please continue holding.
Our representatives are busy helping other customers.
Your wait time is 10 minutes.
Please don't hang up! Please stay on the line.
If you know your party's extension number,
you may dial it at any time.
If you need assistance, say "representative".
Listen to the following options, as our menu has changed.
We'll be with you momentarily.

Your call did not go through. Please try again.
If you need assistance, please dial the operator.
Thank you for continuing to hold.
You dialed too few digits. Please try again.
Please hold while we connect your call.
Sorry! Our office hours are 9 am to 4:30 pm.
Please call again.
If you care to participate in a brief survey,
please remain on the line.

But what to do but go along,
even listening to the music's tune,
and hope to talk to a real live soul,
because dinner is scheduled soon!

Wandering Mind

Do me some harm, or do as I like:
a cuddle or cudgel's your choice.
If friendly or foe, let's keep the status quo
and let peace prevail with one voice.

When buying a poodle, you must use your noodle,
the very whole kit and kaboodle.
You don't want to pay oodles, so don't sit there with doodles.
Be frugal and just try to Google.

The boys were in a huddle, in the middle of a puddle,
trying to befuddle their foe.
Their feeble attempts and efforts so muddled
proved they couldn't run or throw.

There once was a kitty who got lost in the city
and was nowhere to be found.
It really was a pity, but the owner was witty
and immediately called the pound.
She made up a ditty about her nice kitty
which wandered away in the street.
It turned out real ducky, the owner was lucky,
the lost kitty came home, which was neat!

Salesmen Beware

For crying out loud and well, well, well,
gee whiskers and my, oh, my;
oh, brother and a whatchamacallit,
whiz-bang and a good college try!

Ye Gads, and all the little fishes;
by golly and now, now, now;
Jiminy Cricket, you betcha, wink, wink,
hee-haw I cannot allow!

By heck and c'mon and check-mate, too,
come again and get out here!
It's yak,yak,yak and yadda,yadda, yadda,
complain and you can kiss my rear!

You think you're a shoo-in to bring home the bacon,
but don't be so hi-falootin!
If so, you're good for a laugh or two
(and watch your intake of glutin).

You're full of beans and hot air too;
and don't try to pull my leg.
So you may as well git! while the gitin's good,
or else for mercy you'll beg!

A lot of baloney we cannot abide,
A real lemon we'll know by the smell.
A monkey's uncle we try not to be,
Just go and try another to sell!

NEEDS

He did not drink liquor and did not smoke.
He went to bed early for sleep.
He drank lots of water and avoided fats and sweets
and exercised so his physique he could keep.

He ate only veggies and threw tantrums at meat.
His pressure was ideal for his age.
He tried to avoid stress with his diet controlled,
It was a daily battle to wage.

But there's more to life's health than these things above
and thinking he's done all he can.
The spirit and soul need attentions as well,
giving meaning and pleasure (God's plan).

We humans are not solely our physical selves,
standing apart from nature's rest:
our artistic and cultural needs must be met
if we are to enjoy life at its best.

The phrase body and soul has meaning to me,
for all arts lend meaning and depth..
The peace of our soul is a dimension beyond food,
as long as life gives us breath.

City Scene

A look-see of an unfettered soul
sees red kerchief and green wrap
(and possible black thoughts)
before canyoned city facades,
orange hair (once innocent brown);
a colorful nimbus surrounding sun-juiced tan,
marred by circlets of silver enhancing
nostril and ears, and, God help us, tongue;
and, surely, those not-to-be probed
hidden parts beneath sweater and fleece.

Beltless blue denims with scarred and windowed knees
touch thong sandals near an overturned hat
with a single bill and several coins
in front of where she stands.

The guitar's twangy rhythm surrounds
and pulsates the still, breezy air:
and the repetitious smacking of wood
overwhelms whatever her singing lyrics were.

Nearby, in gray jacket with uprolled sleeves
is, surely, a fellow traveling consort
whose visible arms exhibit a tattooer's art.
He sits cross legged and in the fading light
reads a book concealed behind a scribbled card
requesting sympathetic alms.

What made-up story can the majority of strident walkers
conjure in scenario speculation?

Lecture

Thank you for such a great introduction.
It's a pleasure to join you today.
I'm glad you could make it in spite of the rain
to hear what I have to say.

It's my favorite subject and yours too, I hope;
I've studied the question for years!
I've written ten books, and married three times,
and have argued and fought with my peers.

Opinions may vary, with all due respect,
and to be perfectly frank,
there's no question about it, you can check it yourself,
I am considered a crank.
But without skipping a beat or slowing one bit,
my conclusions all add up to this:
this planet was made from angel dust and fried eggs,
and came to life with a kiss.

Those huge beasts with teeth and fiery breath
were debris from the Devil's domain.
They were friendly with Adam and ate jelly beans
and intruded on Eve's green terrain.

Mosquitoes were larger than buildings today
and Noah knew nothing of boats.
It was a big steamship that survived the big flood,
and he failed math, so there were five goats.

Flowers were huge and tied in bouquets
and daisies had only four petals.
Watches were plastic and couldn't tell time,
because there weren't any metals.

The Sunnis and Hutus took pride in the skills,
(the Taliban also joined in)
in settling old scores and sparing no one,
without notifying next of kin.

So ask my opinion, I'll share all as I see it
(Oh, the years I've spent searching for truth!)
like the green elves and their minions and thirty foot pups,
surrounding their red Queen called Ruth.

The whole story is there scratched in rock and in caves,
if one were to know where to look.
If you want to know more and learn truth from the source,
for you, I have just the book!

There are more stones to look under and paths to explore;
my next book will be in five years.
Will our future be safe and secure, you might ask?
Whatever I say there'll be jeers.

Slanguage

When you complained to the big maha,
the big cheese,
(which I just heard about over the grapevine
while shmoozing with the boys)
they say he was boiling mad and flew off the handle:
You touched his hot button.
It's a real hot potato.
I hope you're not in a pickle, or in a jam.
It's funny how everything can go to pot.
Don't bug him. Speak to him again.
Don't get cold feet.
He knows his onions. Butter him up.
Chew on it!
Is there too much on your plate?
I hope you will not be in hot water.
But take it on the chin!
I feel for you. I'm in your corner.
Don't throw in the towel!
He may give you a break. He doesn't horse around!
No how!
If he goes bananas and hits the ceiling,
and gets all out of shape,
it'll cost you an arm and a leg,
but stand by your guns. And don't shoot from the hip.
It's a once-in-a-blue-moon chance
to bring home the bacon,
and have him eating out of your hand.
Don't screw up! I'm not just whistling Dixie.
Everything will be hunky-dory!
No malarkey!
Or whatever!

Pleasures

He was a cute little boy with a joyous laugh,
an adorable grandchild of mine;
alert and bright and curious and smart,
and drew Superman with a cartoonish line.

We picked blueberries together and swam in the lake
and on visits we went on our walk.
Grandma and Grandpa just beamed with our love;
we'd play or would only just talk.

With each calendar year he'd grow and develop:
we'd watch and see him get taller.
That cute kid was becoming a studious young man,
while Grandma and Grandpa got smaller.

My quiet reminiscing brings all this to mind:
Because he graduates from college next week.
We've had joy in the journey from baby to grad,
So there may be a tear on my cheek.

Somebody's Bad Day

"My skin is cold and both feet ache,
my muscles have lost their mass.
My eyesight's failing and my hearing's gone:
how long before I pass?

My bowels are upset, my breathing's wheezy;
I toss uncomfortably all night.
Warm milk won't help; my pills need more space:
old age is such a blight:

I'm losing hair on top, as anyone can see,
but it's filled my nose and ears.
My joints are not my friends anymore,
victims of rusty gears.

My pressure's high, I can't taste food;
I go two or three time a night.
Arthritis is no pal of mine;
my youth is out of sight!

The TV drugs have me in mind:
they brag about their cure.
I've tried them all, but they don't help:
my goose is cooked, for sure!

So, moan and groan does me no good;
my friends all complain like me.
If you don't know some cure for age,
then just you let me be!"

The old man paused, and took a deep breath;
I wasn't sure how to reply.
Was this awaiting me and my fate?
Some day, would I be this guy?

Forgetful

"There are irksome words that rattle me so,
and make me doubt myself:
some words that hurt and do me ill,
discarding me on a shelf.

I try my best, I really do,
with the very best of intention.
It's just not any fault of mine
if I have faulty memory retention!

"Why didn't you…?" and "You really should have…",
"How could you?" and "You did what?".
"How come?" and "Do you mean to tell me…?"
are questions that make my blood clot!

"Oh, no!" and "Whatever were you thinking?"
and "I can't believe you did that!"
Plus "Don't you ever do that again".
I feel like some juvenile brat!

The tempo picks up with "OK, that does it!"
and "What do you mean, you forgot?"
and "Are you an idiot?" and "I told you so!"
I just want to cry in my cot!

"Didn't you realize?" and "Have you lost your mind?"
and "Wherever were your brains?"
"You shouldn't have!" and "How could this happen?"
My ego disappears down the drains!"

I listened intently at my friend's pitiful tale,
and felt sorry for his ego's decline;
Occasionally, we're all forgetful at times:
I told him we're all human, not divine!

He thanked me for my consoling words
and we shook hands to say good-bye.
Then he called me by a different name,
confusing me with another guy!

Young Memories

When I was young and Coney Island my home,
I'd follow the pattern of many a kid.
We'd wait for the summer season to start,
seeking work like my sister did.

We'd make the rounds at games and rides,
at parking lots and fast food stands,
selling cotton candy or cones,
offering ourselves as needed hands.

The boardwalk jobs were the deluxe ones:
they paid the most and had rank:
as server, barker, hawker or shill,
it provided us with money to bank.

Over several years of dong this,
I learned to be unafraid of a crowd.
You couldn't be bashful when trying to sell,
you were expected to be persuasive and loud.

It was a good experience overcoming being shy,
handling change and doing your job.
Some of the food I remembered I sold
was fudge and corn on the cob.

Ice cream custard and saltwater taffy,
hot dogs on a bun with fries;
caramelized popcorn and cold juicy drinks,
while chasing away annoying flies!

Jobs varied with seasons and are part of my past:
and helped build confidence and poise,
But the price that I paid denied me my fun:
playing and swimming with the other boys.

This fragment of biography I think about often;
everyone has their own stories to tell,
of early events that shaped who they are now,
helping personality to define and jell.

Final Yummy

If I had only one last meal to have,
there's no doubt as to what it would be.
I'd hanker for a hot corned beef on rye,
and a half-sour pickle for me!

Hot pastrami is next and a knockwurst or two,
with sauerkraut and mustard, as well.
I'd face gladly my fate, for now I'd be happy,
as I encounter jealousy in hell.

Transition

Old age is really over-rated:
I can't over-emphasize that enough.
Nobody wants to be "over the hill",
but, fighting it is going to be tough!

There's no way to turn the odometer back
to younger times and days.
We've run the course and reaped what's given.
Age signals the end of our maze.

We watch the young and clever move in,
changing all that we've known
It's their time at bat: I hope they do better,
and try ending our world's moan.

But, for me, there is much yet to do and accomplish,
and more thoughts yet to share.
as long as breath and energy allow:
now, that's not an unworthy prayer!

Remembrance Bench

It is touching to read the plaques
attached to the backs of the wooden benches
scattered throughout. New York's Central Park.

Pausing to read the etched messages
is to share the emotions of those who arranged
for such memorials to departed ones:
a family member, friend, mentor.

Or the inscription message might merely be
an expression of the joy that this park
had brought to the plaque sponsor.

For the most part, the inscriptions are
a remembrance expressing love or affection
or thankfulness, or the description of some event.

Each small metal plaque is a bench dedication
available for a fee.

My wife and I have our own special bench
with a plaque that shares a personal history,
bringing smiles to our children and grandchildren.

It tells the curious that on this particular bench,
I sat one night, beneath trees and a moon,
with the girl I was later to marry,
sharing the final moments before embarking overseas
during World War II.

We revisit this particular bench often,
and after sixty-four married years,
I hope it gives rest and pleasure to others.

And it is a story we both are happy to share.

Commonality

From our self-centered viewing of our popular culture,
we believe we have originated pop;
that disco and torrid are fruits of our pulse
with no antecedent to top.

But, recently, an urn, bemossed and unglazed,
was, by chance, unearthed and reviewed,
and proved to hold parchments that shocked and amused,
which pedants and scholars called lewd.

We thought, in our hubris, that our poetry and songs,
reflected words uniquely our own;
but this discovered vessel proved, without doubt,
how common affections are shown.

Our libidinous drives are human, we know,
with desire unrestrained and not coy;
so, unsurprisingly then, these translations inform,
of encounters' appeals and joys:

"Bestir my embers and agitate my decorum,
overwhelm my lassitude.
Spark and beguile, say languor begone!
and be besotted with my gratitude!"

"Let's be drawn into the oblivion of the unknown,
entwined in ecstatic caress,
sparking physical adulation,
knowing that Olympians will bless."

"Oh, be gone this field of mortal fright,
let's reverse time's dropping sand.
Unpower societal shackles and reserve,
and kiss euphoria's hand."

"If we should slide off this earth's flat plane
into Hades' abyss,
that price of oblivion and the unknown
would be tempered by your stolen kiss."

Those words ring true as if written today;
those impulses are so similar to ours.
Thus, we of today must glance back and admire
such universal attractions and powers.

So, "Light my fire!" and "Bring it on, Baby!"
are what we might say today;
not in cultivated prose or in poetic rhymes,
like that old-fashioned erudite way.

A Great Idea

It's a wide open field for some entrepreneur type
to make his mark on this earth:
to bring to the market a product so needed,
that can be not less than rebirth.

When observing a playground with children at play,
the air is alive with their shouts.
They run and jump and put us to shame:
they're the "ins" and we are the "outs".

The energy flows without a pause;
there must be a physical source.
If we could invent one and offer it for sale,
there's a fortune to be made, of course.

We'll call it a battery, easy to install,
like autos and flashlights or toy:
reliable, replaceable, defying time's toll,
energizing like a young girl or boy.

Because my suggestion is now offered here,
I'll be happy for royalties received.
I'll even provide logos and write all the copy.
We aged would be so relieved!

When this is available, I'll be the first to buy
and say, "Hey, kids, let me play, too!"
I'd get off the couch and run a few laps;
(Now, if I only had teeth to chew!)

Gallery Talk

She stares at me with one blue eye,
her foot is curved askew;
her torso tilts and seems so odd,
just like a drunkard's stew.

The breast is where the ear should be:
her nose is on her belly.
The colors seem to beg forgiveness,
and the paint just drips like jelly.

Her teeth are stained (if they are teeth),
a hat is on a chair.
A buttock fills the lower half;
I think the green's her hair.

The frame is saying "Don't blame me,
it's not any fault of mine.
I just surround whatever's there.
Let others say it's fine!".

Home Spun

All in all and on the whole.
whatever and none-the-less;
by golly, shucks and as it were,
are included speech's dress.

For crying out loud and fancy that!
Far-fetched and sakes alive;
be-all, end-all, to a fault:
all this is speakers' jive.

Far and away and a big fat chance
that speech like this will end!
And so it goes, as I make my point,
we cannot stop this blend.

It's belly up and shake a leg,
gee whiskers and bite your tongue.
I'll see you around and toodle-oo,
I feel crummy and high strung.

So, lo and behold and gosh, darn it,
gee whiz and on second thought,
don't try to change the way we talk.
It would be all for naught!

Dig?

Separate Lives

The blinds, disturbed by errant breeze,
intruded as I lay,
and sought to join my half-waked brain
without an "If I may".

It wants to share my stupor's tale
that makes no sense with dawn;
what seemed so real in slumbered state
now brings a puzzled yawn.

The actors played with scenic change,
who knows the plots that flow:
the chase, the scares, the caves, the fright,
all go with dawning's glow.

The scenes seemed real, I can recall,
a strange sequenced parade:
a mix of remembered acts and casts,
to create this night's charade.

I look around for a solid grasp
and try to calm my senses.
The space between what's real and dream
depends so much on fences!

Reality is a life awake,
with familiar scene and folk;
the dividing fence between wake and doze
defines the darkness cloak.

Theory

So much has been written and taken as true
about male and female traits,
that causes abound to explain what we think
accounts for some differing fates.

Over some years I've pondered the issue,
seeking the secret of man's role.
Was it a matter of efforts learned well,
or nature's thoughtful goal?

I've thought long and hard to puzzle this out,
and weighed reasons for man's dominion.
The answer I've found may surprise and amuse,
and is, of course, only my opinion.

The clothes that males wear, whether pants or a coat,
have spaces that we all call pockets,
which hold, store, carry and collect,
while females have frills and her lockets.

All such self-contained aids go wherever he goes,
whether keys, coins, papers and more;
whatever is needed, wallet or comb,
those pockets are handy to store.

So, laugh if you must, but you'll see that I'm right:
just ask me to show what I carry.
The riddle is solved, I've discovered the truth.
My brilliance sometimes is so scary!

Body-Speak

It's hard to talk with tongue in cheek,
or when I say a mouthful.
I scratch my head in wonderment:
to crack a smile is doubtful.

When snubbed, I turn the other cheek.
I take it on the chin.
I'm all ears when you tell a joke:
your humor brings a grin.

So, take a deep breath and stand up straight;
and I hope you can take a ribbing.
If you were to look me straight in the eye,
you'll know I'm not just fibbing.

You arch your brows and tilt your head;
you shrug your shoulders, too.
I know you cannot stomach fools,
whose features leave no clue.

Stop pulling my leg or twisting my arm;
instead use elbow grease.
If it doesn't cost an arm and a leg,
I guess I'll sign the lease.

So much of speech are body parts;
I'm here at your call and beck.
Take my advice and put nose to stone,
and don't be a pain in the neck!

Season's Home

Master of this garden's view,
the oldest growth in sight,
with darkened bark and outstretched arms,
this tree expresses might.

Those arms invite and say "hello",
it wants to hug, I know:
at least they offer perch to friends
who bask and frolic so.

The feathered neighbors roost and chat
amidst the sun's descent,
holding firm on comfort's bough,
and paying chirps as rent.

The leaves conceal and shield from breeze
as darkness envelops all,
and joins with limbs as embracing kin,
until the coming fall.

But before the chill and snow and storm,
the tree still gives its most:
the vacated branch is a home once more
and becomes some squirrel's host.

Enough Is Enough

I'll never forget that last trip I took,
as a tourist in beautiful Rome,
traveling on a tour bus with others like me
to see sights so different from home.

Our group was diverse, as such groups are,
composed of all walks of life:
some erudite, curious, gabby and awed,
some single, or husband and wife.

The tour guide was a friendly man,
and patiently showed us the sights:
the buildings and streets and art by the mile,
a proud Roman sharing his delights.

So went the days of our wonderful time,
until one day his demeanor burst wild.
This mild-mannered, scholarly and cultured gent
experienced what made him so riled.

He had saved the last day for the best of the tour:
the Sistine, Michelangelo's best:
but two of the women preferred not to join.
They had come to buy a leather vest!

Fellow Soldiers

A crazy thought popped into my head
upon looking at a General's jacket,
with all its colorful ribbons and bars,
and displaying hierarchy's bracket.

It could be an honor, deed or event,
or identifying group or status;
each will announce with recognizable ease
one's past and present, for gratis.

Now, imagine each one of us doing the same
with ribbons or emblems to wear,
informing another of battles we've fought
and events we might want to share.

Our trials and successes and losses and pain
(not forgetting our accomplishments, too!)
can be visually shared, each ribbon or sign,
announcing what we have been through!

Each star for a victory, each color for deeds,
a medal for rising from a fall;
an epaulet for coping, an insignia for love,
or answering parenting's call.

We'd know at a glance that wearer's trials,
and see who might merit salutes:
victors over pain or conquest of fear,
deserving drums and flutes!

Bountiful Buffet

I just love the choices of a major buffet,
where dozens of foods are laid out,
awaiting selection and replenishments, too,
regardless of heartburn or gout.

Tray after tray all neatly lined up
are piled high with a generous hand;
some steaming or fried or simmering in juice:
bountiful fruits of the land.

The portions are large or neatly arranged
awaiting choice and selection.
Repeat visits are expected and indeed this is so:
no one needs any direction.

Fish, flesh or fowl, or soups and desserts:
it's a hungering mouth's delight.
It's a shower of plenty for a relative pittance
and a fantasist's obscene sight.

But my guilt is the condiment as I pick up my plate,
for I think of some parts of the earth.
Here I am gorging while others are hungry:
such disparity is absurd and no mirth!

It's a sobering thought, unpleasantly intrusive,
for bountiful buffets should be shared.
I hope that one day our dreams are fulfilled:
as if somebody really cared!

Mexican Hayride

I cannot forget what happened long ago
that keeps recurring at many odd times.
I refer to an almost disastrous event
that might have prevented my passion for rhymes.

I had just gotten married and went on a trip
to Mexico City with my bride.
I was enrolled in a summer school studying art;
we would take a honeymoon ride.

We'd spend two months and start memory's book
together in an exotic location.
It would be study and fun and adventure for us
in that strange yet nearby nation.

So, that summer slipped by with a bull fight or two,
until it was time to pack.
We had gotten a ride down from the north,
now, how would we get safely back?

So, I posted a note with a funny face
seeking to thumb a ride;
and sure enough back came a response:
a jalopy and swallowing pride!

It was an ancient auto with no functioning wipers:
it had seen lots of better days.
But, since return we must, we agreed to the deal;
we were young and game in our ways.

The driver was burly and thoughtful and friendly
with a dog as friendly as well.
We all fitted snugly, easily conversing,
unmindful of the coming hell!

We made good time, without a breakdown
on roads not in the best shape.
Cecil, our driver, we learned as we went,
was addicted to his distilled grape.

The tires held out, so no complaints there,
but the weather was giving us hints.
The sky then opened with its wettest deluge,
and filled with blackish tints.

But, imagine a car in a pouring rain
without windshield wipers to wipe!
By now the roads were slippery and soggy –
I embraced my wife whispering "Yipe!".

So, panic-stricken at skidding off a cliff,
with no visibility to steer,
slipping and sliding at the mercy of Fate,
I'd say there was reason for fear!

continued…

To add to this trio's discomfort and fright,
another element intruded:
we looked at each other with silent suspicion,
since odor was now being exuded!

We finally determined, with social relief
that the dog was the mischief-maker,
compounding all our other woes and scares
as an additional comfort taker.

The wind-driven rain pelted the wiper-less car;
we were helpless and the danger was clear.
Our hopes for our futures were fast fading away:
We'd give anything for New York to be near!

But, somehow our ends were just not to be,
for with a joy and thankful relief,
we made it back home, and said our good-byes,
not referring to our adventure and grief.

So, here I sit, having remembered it all,
an experience that taught me well:
to always ride with air-conditioning and wipers
so I wouldn't have such stories to tell.

Let's Reminisce

Please come to my party and say hello to old times.
Let's gather for our last good-bye.
Let's see the faces we looked at before,
and talk about our past with a sigh.

Let's reminisce and joke about the fun that we shared,
and those characters that we can recall:
the habits and opinions we laughed at and mocked,
and some things that now we appall.

Let me look once more at the days of my youth,
before time's curtain finally drops down.
And if you're unable to join, wish me well…
I'll give your regards to the clown.

Winner Take All

There's one word that I would love to say often
in a very loud and distinct way,
that creates a hushed awe and even applause:
I'd like to elaborate, if I may.

I'm a man who likes numbers and games of all sorts,
and I've played whenever I can;
but there's one game with odds that I cannot control,
although I've tried every strategy and plan.

I've studied the concept and have occasionally won.
I've mastered all the moves and the lingo:
and I'll keep playing and trying until my last day,
until I hear myself shouting "BINGO!".

Some Observations

He helped write the law that governs your trade
and oversees your business ways;
and now, for a fee, he will join up with you
to help you outsmart the maze.

Our Congress, elected to represent us
and oversee our welfare and need,
sometimes respond to special interests that pay:
for re-election is in bed with greed.

Political influence may take many forms,
from junkets and over-paid speeches.
These actions are hidden and some come to light,
as many a newscast teaches.

The lobbying troops that glut up the halls,
very often are lawmakers, now available,
whose former friends provide easy access
with such influence being highly saleable.

Media for messages are persuasive, but costly,
and tend to be dominated by a few.
So, influence is weighted and public interest is thwarted.
Now tell me: What else is new?

Abra-Cadabra

Oh, those nimble fingers and rabbit in hat;
the white dove that flies without source.
Those scarves with hues, like rainbow nymphs
that magically appear, of course.

The awesome skill of picking the card;
those fingers that flawlessly choose.
I'm a child who shamelessly is impressed
at every trick and ruse.

That beautiful blond who enters that box,
and then is stabbed with swords:
but despite the cruelty of such a scene
emerges to the relief of the hordes.

We'll always love magic: the voila! and hocus-pocus,
the tensions provoked by illusion.
We forget for a moment our reality-based lives
and appreciate the world of delusion.

If only with a word or waving a wand
we could also make trouble disappear;
at that moment, at least, we'd master our lives,
but reality is too smart, I fear!

Idiom Fever

I'm in a quagmire and in a dither,
I'm in a stew and a daze.
I'm really on pins and needles, as well,
on so many levels and ways.

I need a moment to collect my thoughts,
for everything's up in the air.
It's hip, hip, hooray and pie in the sky,
and I've already paid my fare.

It's catch as catch can, for I'm out of the loop.
I'm ready to go with the flow.
You're a barrel of laughs and ahead of the game:
I knew you'd go for the dough.

I'm on to you, so don't pull my leg,
or I'll hit the ceiling for sure!
Don't fly off the handle or eat like a pig;
and collecting your wits is the cure.

You think you have pull or can skirt the issue;
if so, it's beyond belief.
So, pack it in, we're all in the same boat:
it's a humdinger, and that's a relief!

With foresight and hindsight, it's right on the button;
it's the best bet far and away.
I've bent over backwards, and am pleased as punch,
and I'm happy to have had my say.

Tipping Point

One by one, it has been reported,
that some creatures are fewer or gone.
Our streams are polluted or murky at best,
and rocks no longer have frogs on.

The numbers of butterflies that were once seen
have steadily reduced, to our shame.
Even bees and some birds no longer visit,
victims of our short-sighted game.

Nor are we humans safe and immune,
for diseases and deaths have increased.
Common sense and controls have long been ignored;
if continued, life will have ceased.

So, flowers and sunshine and meandering brooks,
while pretty and soulful to describe,
are not the only subjects for poets who write,
for living and slow death do not jibe!

Sad Snapshot

Imagine the travesty and a political jest
of a title like "President For Life"!
Elections, if any, are shams and deceits,
and corruption and nepotism rife.

The land's natural resources and anything of value
are usurped for family and cronies.
The juice of any riches are sucked up and gathered,
and distributed among the uniformed and phonies.

It's pitiful and sad to think of our world
in this twenty-first century just begun;
no matter the titles these strongmen who rule,
they wield the power of cruelty and gun.

Pyramid

Of all the sights engraved in mind,
there's one that still brings a smile:
it's a little girl sitting atop her dad,
an image still tagged in my file.

Of course, we've seen dads with kids aloft,
but this was a special scene:
for the little girl carried her own doll atop,
sharing fun, queen atop queen.

When I Was A Boy

Some early memories cling like burrs
and recur and won't let go.
In idle moments they reappear,
but I don't mind if that's so.

Some vivid scenes are still fresh in mind
and cause a grin or two;
bittersweet thoughts of years gone by,
when life was fresh and new.

I remember when my hair was cut
before school in the fall.
The barber gave a special gift:
a Spalding rubber ball.

Another gift was a pencil box,
if shoes were bought, as well.
Some even had a pull-out drawer
(still remembered as you can tell).

The charlotte russe was the king of treats,
the Eskimo Pie was, too.
The candies in the glass showcase
to suck, or bite or chew.

A penny bought a tasty snack:
the choices made heads swim.
The landlord's son had three cents to spend:
he lived life to the brim!

Some Thoughts On This Day

(A Speech On A Granddaughter's Wedding)

On this wonderful day when wedding and vows
will be remembered in all coming years,
a journey begins on one of life's roads,
with helpings of laughter and tears.

Destiny's hand was surely involved,
and Fate's touch led to this hour,
this beautiful pair , now man and wife,
can now rest in their romantic bower.

Life undulates so with highs and lows;
with smooth miles and some bumpy patches.
But steering's the trick with wipers that work,
and troubles will have found their matches.

There'll be moments of hurts and challenge and stress:
almost everyone's had such to endure.
Love and trust will surely ease the path:
these are things of which we are sure.

But if one were to ask what the one secret would be
for a union that will yield the most fruit,
it's allowing and respecting each other's space,
with resilience and patience, to boot.

The pleasures of friendship will season the way,
a sharing of good with the bad;
enjoying each other's humor and mirth:
that's the advice from grand-mom and grand-dad.

Visions

Those fanciful figures, alive in my head,
cavorting and dancing with ease:
high kicks and arms swaying, torsos atwisting,
as if my aloneness to appease.

The wordless swirl of shadowy shapes
reminds me of a revelry's romp,
whose abandon and fervor help escape from the staid
untying the laces of pomp.

My art also responds and echoes the scene,
flirting with creativity's drive;
and duplicates the blueprint noiselessly inside,
emphasizing that I am alive!

About The Author

Nathan Polsky, author of two volumes of poetry, *Meaningful Sounds* and *Bountiful Buffet*, is a native New Yorker. He has been married for over sixty-four years to a woman with whom he attended their high school prom. They have two daughters.

He was an elementary school art teacher, cartoonist, illustrator, fabric designer and artist. His work appeared in various newspapers and periodicals. He won an award from the New York Art Directors Club for a work commissioned by CBS. He is still a working artist.

During World War II, he was a bombardier, flying over two dozen missions, earning a Purple Heart and two Bronze Stars.

Polsky has a BS and an MA degree from NYU. His professional career included being Director of several community arts organizations, Project Director at Macmillan and Houghton Mifflin publishers, and advertising manager with several paper companies.

He founded and was president of Scratch-Art Co., an arts and crafts company, inventing and manufacturing many original creative art products for schools and commercial markets before finally selling the company and retiring.

For the last several years, he has concentrated on writing poems, focusing on personal thoughts, observations, experiences, memories, etc. seeing the serious and humorous sides of life.

Previously Published By Nathan Polsky

MEANINGFUL SOUNDS: New and Collected Poems,
© 2013, Suncoast Digital Press, Inc.

Available at Barnes & Noble online and Amazon.com (eBook and Paperback versions)

Suncoast Digital Press, Inc. is a publishing company in Sarasota, Florida. For more information on this author or other books published by Suncoast Digital Press, Inc., please visit www.SuncoastDigitalPress.com.

Below: A sample from Nathan Polsky's first volume of poetry, *Meaningful Sounds.*

Passing Encounter

I love to see the head of a dog
sticking out, taking in sights
through the rolled down window of a passing car,
claiming its canine rights.

He tries to make contact as we ride side by side
from his chauffeured, coddled nook.
The wind roughs up his hair, his eyes glistening so
with a "I-want-to-get-to-know-you" look.

Sometimes, I notice an "I'm somebody!"stare,
on an adventure so memorable and fine.
A brief friendship can flourish as our moving eyes lock
between his open window and mine.

www.ingramcontent.com/pod-product-compliance
Lightning Source LLC
Chambersburg PA
CBHW070641050426
42451CB00008B/258
9781939237187